BORN OF A WOMAN

A STUDY GUIDE FOR INDIVIDUALS AND SMALL GROUPS

Born of a Woman

A BISHOP RETHINKS THE BIRTH OF JESUS

John Shelby Spong

A STUDY GUIDE FOR INDIVIDUALS AND SMALL GROUPS
BY JUDITH L. HEGG

HarperSanFrancisco
An Imprint of HarperCollins*Publishers*

Biblical quotations are from the *Revised Standard Version* of the Bible
and the *New Standard Version* of the Bible.

BORN OF A WOMAN: *A Study Guide for Individuals and Small Groups.*
Copyright © 1995 by HarperCollins. All rights reserved. Printed in the
United States of America. No part of this book may be used or repro-
duced in any manner whatsoever without written permission except in
the case of brief quotations embodied in critical articles and reviews.
For information address HarperCollins Publishers, 10 East 53rd Street,
New York, NY 10022.

HarperCollins®, 📖®, and HarperSanFrancisco™ are trademarks of
HarperCollins Publishers Inc.

FIRST EDITION

Study Guide ISBN 0–06–067540–3

Library of Congress Cataloging-in-Publication Data
Spong, John Shelby
Born of a woman: a bishop rethinks the birth of Jesus / John Shelby
Spong. — 1st ed.
p.   cm.
Includes bibliographical references and index.
ISBN 0–06–067513–6 (alk. paper)
ISBN (intl.) 0–06–067529–2
1. Jesus Christ—Nativity. 2. Bible. N.T.—Criticism, interpretation,
etc. I. Title.
BT315.2.S66 1992
232.92'1—dc20   91–55087
                                                              CIP

95 96 97 98 99 ❖ VICKS 10 9 8 7 6 5 4 3 2 1

CONTENTS

PROFILE OF THE RIGHT REVEREND
JOHN SHELBY SPONG

John Shelby Spong, author of fourteen books and more than seventy published articles, is a bishop in the Episcopal Church. His writings and extensive media appearances have made him a household name in his own denomination and a sought-after lecturer and guest speaker in Protestant circles on several continents as well as in some Roman Catholic communities.

Bishop Spong was born in 1931 in Charlotte, North Carolina, and was educated in the public schools of that city. He graduated Phi Beta Kappa in 1952 from the University of North Carolina at Chapel Hill and received his Master of Divinity degree in 1955 from the Protestant Episcopal Theological Seminary in Virginia. Both that seminary and St. Paul's College have conferred on him honorary Doctor of Divinity degrees. He served as rector of two parishes in North Carolina between 1955 and 1965, and two parishes in Virginia from 1965 to 1976. In 1976 he was consecrated bishop coadjutor of the Diocese of Newark and became the diocesan bishop in 1979.

The Bishop speaks openly of his love for the holy Scriptures, which he traces to a Christmas gift of a Bible that he received as a young boy. Early daily reading of this book and later study and research laid the foundation for his interest in Christian education. All of his Southern pastorates as well as his episcopate have had as their hallmarks his crusade for high-quality adult Christian education. His willingness to discuss his views in high-profile situations has led to national television coverage of debates with noted biblical conservatives such as Jerry Falwell and Episcopal Bishop William Wantland as well as a videotaping with Anglican author and scholar John R. W. Stott of London.

Unafraid to sail into uncharted waters, Bishop Spong has seen many of his books and other writings unleash storms of protest and outrage. For instance, his 1988 book *Living in Sin?* was born in controversy. Scheduled for publication by Abingdon Press, the denominational publisher of the United Methodist Church, the book was canceled three weeks before its release date as potentially too divisive. Picked up by Harper & Row and brought to publication just before the Episcopal Church's 1988 general convention, which would be discussing whether practicing homosexuals should be ordained, the book became an immediate best-seller. Within weeks Bishop Spong had been interviewed on fifteen television programs, five of them on national networks, and twenty-one radio shows.

Bishop Spong continues to be seen on national television as his views on the biblical birth narratives, the resurrection, the literal understanding of the Bible, and issues of sexuality are debated in the public arena. He challenges the traditional standards of the church in both his writings and his lectures, bringing many persons long ignored by the church back into its fold. The dialogue he has initiated continues.

He says about *Born of a Woman*, "This book is important to me because I see what western Christianity has done to women, primarily through the eyes of my daughters. They are all professional women: a bank vice president, a lawyer, a research physicist, and a chemical engineer. The stereotype that has come through the church defines women in terms of their biology and even there it tends to cover the biology of a female with a sense of compromise and shame. In my effort to break that stereotype, to open the doors of both the church and the society to the full participation by women in every aspect of life, I found the Bible in general and the portrait of the Virgin in particular being used as weapons of oppression. So in this book I sought to raise these issues to consciousness.

"Beyond that, it is my experience that if one literalizes the stories of virgin births, angels singing to hillside shepherds, and magi following stars, one turns Christianity into something far less than what I believe it is. So I wanted to lay claim to the truth behind these birth legends for those modern people who have tended to dismiss these stories and to use that truth to empower people, especially women, to enter into the fullness of their humanity. This book might well be my personal favorite."

PURPOSE OF THE STUDY GUIDE

Born of a Woman: A Bishop Rethinks the Birth of Jesus is a fresh, provocative, and perhaps daring, look at the birth narratives of the Gospels of Matthew and Luke as well as speculation on how they have shaped the church and our society. The author fully intended this book to open debate on the issues he raises. Therefore, the Study Guide is designed first to assist you, the reader, in understanding the author's major points and supportive documentation. A second and equally important purpose, however, is to enable and encourage you to articulate your own feelings and arguments about the issues the bishop has raised. These two goals are accomplished primarily by incorporating five activities into the reading of the individual chapters: (1) reading a summary of a specific chapter, (2) reading biblical passages noted by the author as applicable to these pages, (3) documenting new insights the specific chapter and the accompanying biblical material have generated for you, (4) answering discussion questions, and (5) recording in a journal or notebook any personal feelings that the material has engendered. The journal, particularly, is expected to be an integral part of the process as you isolate your own opinions, feelings, and concerns.

DIRECTIONS FOR USING THE STUDY GUIDE

As you begin your study of *Born of a Woman*, you will need to have available a few materials in addition to the book and the Study Guide. First, you should have a copy of either the Revised Standard Version (RSV) of the Bible or the New Revised Standard Version (NRSV). If you have another edition with which you are especially familiar and comfortable, you are urged to use that *in addition* to one of the other two. Second, you will be directed to write in a journal at regular intervals. This journal can be either a loose-leaf notebook or a hardbound book of blank pages. It should, in any case, be durable, since you will be encouraged to return to reread your entries. Third, although not essential, it will be helpful if you have available a Bible dictionary or a similar reference work. A good choice is the *Harper's Bible Dictionary*, which also contains maps of the sites mentioned in *Born of a Woman*. Finally, you should bring an open mind to the admittedly controversial material in this book. Obviously this is not an easy task, but growth and change come from entertaining new and challenging ideas. It may be that you will find your earlier beliefs strengthened, but it may be that they will be modified or perhaps reversed. As you begin your reading, be open to new ideas as they come to you. Do not be afraid to take them in directions previously unexplored by you, but on the other hand, continue to challenge them with your own experience and your own reasoning.

The Study Guide format of each portion of the book will be similar.

1. Begin each study section by reading the appropriate chapter in *Born of a Woman*. Following this you will be directed to read the summary or digest of the material in the Study Guide.

2. In each of the chapters Bishop Spong will have suggested biblical readings to support his arguments. You should at this point locate those biblical references in his writing and find and read them in the Bible you have available. As you read each one, ask yourself

why the author included this reference and if you believe it effectively supports his thesis.

A word about biblical notations: The first numbers after the name of the book from the Bible identify the chapter that is cited; the numbers after the colon are the verses. Therefore, Mark 2 would indicate the entire second chapter of Mark; Mark 2:14 would designate the second chapter of Mark, verse 14; and Mark 2:14–16 would be the second chapter of Mark, verses 14 through 16. Also, some of the books have similar names—differentiated only by their beginning numerals—such as 1 Chronicles and 2 Chronicles. Be certain you are reading the appropriate reference.

3. There follows an opportunity for you to write in the Study Guide any new insights you have acquired in the course of reading the chapter and the biblical references. These insights might include, for example, a new awareness or understanding, a new fact, a new connection, an intriguing image, or a fresh discovery.

4. Next you will be asked to read, think about, and answer the Questions for Reflection in order to get beneath the specific words and examples used by Bishop Spong. If you are using the Study Guide alone, it is suggested that you take the time to write answers to these discussion or reflection questions. If you are proceeding through the material with another person or several people, however, discuss these questions together. This will encourage and stimulate further ideas as you work together.

5. The final step for each chapter is writing in your journal. The framework for this recording will be in the form of a letter, and it is suggested that you write to the same person after each chapter. The individual you select to correspond with should be someone you know—either a friend or a family member—and with whom you would like to share your feelings. You might select someone whose religious views are similar to yours, or someone with polar-opposite views. In any case, your focus for this writing should be on concerns, unanswered questions, and personal feelings about the portion of the material just completed. The purpose of this activity is to encourage you to articulate how the reading has engaged you. Bishop

Spong has anticipated that some of his ideas may surprise or shock you, but some may confuse you as well. And, of course, like many others, you may encounter the pain of discovering personal prejudices of which you were never conscious. When you have finished the book and the Study Guide, you will have in your journal a collection of letters with the personal concerns and feelings the book has evoked. You will certainly know more about Bishop Spong and his theology, but more important, you will also know more about yourself and how you react to ideas that challenge formerly untested convictions or your personal prejudices and biases. Even if you are working with a small group in your study of *Born of a Woman*, it is important that each person keep his or her own journal. There is no need to share these with others unless you choose to do so.

READY TO BEGIN

At this point, open your journal and commence your work by recording a list of your expectations in reading *Born of a Woman* and using the accompanying Study Guide. You will refer to this list when you have finished the book to determine if your goals have been met. Begin now by reading the preface to *Born of a Woman*.

CHAPTER ONE

ESCAPING BIBLICAL LITERALISM

SUMMARY

Bishop Spong sets the stage in this first chapter by clearly stating that his objective in writing *Born of a Woman* is to demonstrate the role that the church and the Bible have played in the oppression of women over the centuries. The method he will use concentrates on the birth narratives about Jesus found in the biblical books of Matthew and Luke. These stories, more than any others in the Bible, have generated a negative influence on women throughout history.

It is necessary, however, to state unequivocally that the author does not interpret the biblical texts for the reader with a literal understanding. Rather, he attempts to get beneath the words to determine what the New Testament writers intended to convey to their first-century audiences.

The expanding knowledge revolution of the past six hundred years has made it difficult for the educated person to continue to regard the literal words of the Bible as inerrant and eternal. These new scientific discoveries in the areas of biology, geology, and astrophysics, for example, have made it appear ludicrous to accept literally such stories as Joshua stopping the sun in its course in order to win the battle against the Amorites, or Jonah's three days in the belly of a great fish, or a seven-day creation as reported in Genesis.

In addition, the common understanding of genetics in the first century assumed the entire life of an infant to be present genetically in the sperm of the male. The woman offered nothing but the womb—an incubator. Thus, if the male were replaced with a divine element, the resulting infant would be divine, not human, a concept that contradicts our understanding of a Jesus who is both fully human and fully divine.

The Bible is also replete with contradictions. A classic example is the commandment from Exodus, "You shall not kill," followed in several places by a directive to kill specific persons. Which is the portion to be believed literally? Also, the God who appears to be a God for all persons—Jew and Gentile alike—as reflected in Malachi is portrayed in Exodus as rejoicing over the drowning of Egyptians in the Red Sea. Again, which, if either, should be interpreted literally?

Further problems face the reader who, in reading the Bible literally, encounters a morality that appears depraved when compared with our own twentieth-century standards. Righteous Lot, for example, offered his virgin daughters to an angry mob in Sodom. And this same literal reading has led over the centuries to prejudices, rejection, and oppression of numerous groups of people. Witness the results of such literal interpretations throughout history on Jews, homosexuals, slaves, and divorced persons. Recall the persecution of pagans and the popularity of the Crusades.

When we study the mythology of other cultures from ancient times, it becomes apparent that many of the most significant Christian symbols are paralleled in these stories. Virgin births, resurrections, and ascensions abound. Yet these stories are read by contemporary people without literalizing. Why can we not read our own religious faith stories the same way?

Is it not possible to read the Bible and understand its great truths without taking it literally? Is it not possible to be postmodern, accepting the new understandings of knowledge in the twentieth century, and still be a Christian? Bishop Spong is offering us a journey to demonstrate that indeed this is possible.

BIBLICAL READINGS

Exodus 20:13	Genesis 7:6–10
1 Samuel 15:3ff.	Mark 6:48–49
Joshua 10:12–13	John 6:1–14
Jonah 1:17	Matthew 27:25
Exodus 14:21ff.	Genesis 19:8
Exodus 16:5	1 Kings 11:3

NEW INSIGHTS

....

....

....

QUESTIONS FOR REFLECTION

1. On page 5 of *Born of a Woman*, Spong notes a number of contradictions in the Bible. Are there any others that you would add to his list? Have these ever disturbed you? How have you accommodated them?

2. Spong states that he does not believe that the story of Mary's virginity has enhanced her portrait. Do you agree?

3. Do you believe that Noah gathered all the animals of the world into the ark? That Jesus walked on water? That the multitude was really fed with five loaves and two fish? Would the stories still be an important part of your faith if they were not literally true? Why or why not?

4. How would you answer a challenger who asked how it is possible to believe in the Bible if you pick and choose what to accept?

5. The author asks if the religious traditions of Christianity can be taken seriously but not literally (p. 12). How would you respond to him?

ACTIVITY

Now begin writing a letter to the person with whom you have chosen to correspond. Reveal the thoughts and concerns you had as you completed this first chapter of Born of a Woman. *If you have unanswered questions, issues you wish Spong had emphasized, or points of disagreement with him, include those as well. Sign and date your letter.*

CHAPTER TWO

APPROACHING THE STORY THROUGH MIDRASH

SUMMARY

There is a method for approaching the Bible that does not require the reader to take a stand at one of two opposite poles of interpretation: believing literally every word written by the biblical writers or rejecting everything since it is all so clearly impossible. This method is called midrash.

An example of the midrashic process takes place, according to the author, with Luke's telling of the ascension and the Pentecost experience. Luke is the only Gospel writer who gives us an account of these two events. In his narration Luke relies heavily on the Elijah of the Hebrew Scriptures, who had become a powerful legend in the religious life of the Jews. Elijah, according to 2 Kings, had bodily ascended into heaven in a chariot of fire drawn by horses of fire, promising his disciple Elisha a double share of his extraordinary spirit if he could see Elijah's actual ascension. Luke, recognizing the power of this story for his Jewish audience, and wishing to demonstrate that Jesus was the new and greater Elijah, had Jesus also ascend to heaven and leave for his followers a sustaining spirit. Note, however, the contrast: Jesus ascended without the need of a chariot and poured out the power of God's Holy Spirit, not on one follower, but upon the gathered Christian community. The fire, a symbol of Elijah from centuries earlier, rested upon the disciples without consuming or harming them. It was another suggestion of Jesus' identity, according to Luke, as a new and greater Elijah.

Midrash, as described by Spong, "represented efforts on the part of the rabbis to probe, tease, and dissect the sacred story looking for hidden meanings, filling in blanks, and seeking clues to yet-to-be-revealed truths" (p. 18). In a sense, the sacred text is seen as timeless and true for all generations—past, present, and future.

Gospel writers were not attempting to answer the oft-heard query, "Is it true?" Rather, they were pursuing the question, "What does all this mean?" It was not objective history nor biography that they were writing but testaments of faith. Over and over in the Gospels, signs of the midrashic tradition appear.

The only historical truth encapsulated in the birth narratives is the fact that Jesus was born. The remainder of the story that surrounds this single simple fact can be interpreted by contemporary readers as efforts by the Gospel writers to understand the power and impact of the adult Jesus on his followers. It took decades for the birth stories to appear in written form. But it was the power of the adult Jesus that created the need for them.

BIBLICAL READINGS

2 Kings 2:11	Acts 2:1ff.
2 Kings 2:15	Matthew 27:3–10
1 Kings 18:20–39	2 Samuel 17:23
2 Kings 1:9–12	Zechariah 11:4–14
Luke 9:54	Luke 7:11–17
Acts 1:1–11	1 Kings 17:17–24

NEW INSIGHTS

....

....

....

QUESTIONS FOR REFLECTION

1. Some writers question whether Spong is correctly using the midrashic tradition in this book. The word *midrash* is defined in *Harper's Bible Dictionary* (1985) as "the type of biblical interpretation found in rabbinic literature. . . . Midrashic interpretation pays close attention to the meanings of individual words and

grammatical forms, elucidates one verse by another verse, and relates the teachings of rabbinic Judaism to the biblical text. Midrash assumes that the biblical text has an inexhaustible fund of meaning that is relevant to and adequate for every question and situation." Do you believe that this definition parallels the description of midrash that Spong gives in this chapter?

2. Does using the midrashic technique to explain portions of the Christian story help you understand these passages? Reread Spong's examples on page 20 as you contemplate this question.

3. What do you think are the identifying marks of a biography? Do you believe that the Gospels fulfill those characteristics? Regardless of your response to that question, do you suppose the first audiences to whom these Gospels were addressed thought of them as "biographies"?

4. Imagine you had been a luncheon guest with the woman who noted that if Bishop Spong were correct, it would mean that Luke was lying (p. 18). How would you have responded to her statement?

5. If neither a literal understanding of the Gospel stories nor the complete abandonment of them was your solution to the difficulties many twentieth-century readers have in their interpretation, how did you satisfy your concerns? Do you find the use of midrash a more persuasive or less persuasive approach than your own?

ACTIVITY

Return to your journal and write a second letter to your correspondent. Enter the emotions you felt as you read chapter 2—were you angered, relieved, confused?—as well as any new insights you wish to share. Once again, sign and date your letter.

CHAPTER THREE

BORN OF A WOMAN—PAUL'S WITNESS

SUMMARY

The apostle Paul, writing some twenty years after the death of Jesus and perhaps twenty years before the appearance of the first Gospel, was not only the most prolific of the New Testament writers but also the earliest. Thus, it is in the letter that Paul wrote to the Christians living in Galatia that we have the earliest written reference to Jesus' birth. There is no mention here of a wondrous conception or birth, simply the words ". . . God sent forth his Son, born of a woman, born under the law. . . ." For Paul, the events surrounding this birth were unexceptional, unimportant, or unknown.

Paul's second and final reference, written perhaps five years later to the Christians in the church at Rome, is also silent on a miraculous birth. The significant words in that letter are ". . . who was descended from David according to the flesh and designated Son of God in power according to the Spirit of holiness by his resurrection. . . ." Once again, there is no mention of a supernatural birth. For Paul, the assumption is a Jesus of unexceptional origins.

In Paul's theology, Jesus was indeed seen to embody a life in which the divine and the human had come inexplicably together. Asserting this, however, did not create the need for an exceptional beginning. In fact, for Paul and the generation of Christians of his day, the religious issues of concern were not related to Jesus' birth but rather to his death. "How could the messiah be crucified?" It was the succeeding generation of Christians who looked to his birth to answer the question of who Jesus was.

BIBLICAL READINGS

Galatians 4:4–5	Acts 12:1–2
Galatians 1:19	Romans 1:3–4
Acts 15	Romans 4:24; 6:9; 10:9

1 Corinthians 15:4, 13–15, 20   Colossians 1:15

Philippians 2:9   Philippians 2:5–11

1 Corinthians 15:13   Matthew 22:42

NEW INSIGHTS

....

....

....

QUESTIONS FOR REFLECTION

1. What are the similarities and differences between the birth stories of Moses and Muhammad? How would you compare them to the stories surrounding Jesus' birth? Why do you imagine these stories have been preserved?

2. Were you aware that Matthew, Mark, Luke, and John were not the first New Testament writings and that Paul wrote his letters almost a generation earlier? Explain the impact of this fact on your understanding of the birth narratives.

3. Do you believe it is possible that Paul knew of a miraculous birth but did not include it in his writings?

4. Do you think greater credence should be given to those biblical authors who wrote closer in time to the events they recalled? For instance, should Paul be given greater authority than Luke when we discuss the origins of Jesus? Why or why not?

5. Reread the paragraph on page 24 about James, the brother of Jesus. Imagine you are reading a detective story. Using the evidence that Spong presents, how would you answer the question he raises concerning the leadership of the church wishing to suppress the identification of James as Jesus' brother?

6. What is a Trinitarian (p. 25)? What evidence does Spong present to support his contention that Paul was *not* a Trinitarian?

ACTIVITY

Return to your journal and start another letter to your correspondent. Be certain to include new information and insights that have created concerns or raised questions that you hope will be satisfied as you continue reading.

CHAPTER FOUR

FROM THE SCANDAL OF THE CROSS TO THE SCANDAL OF THE CRIB

SUMMARY

Jesus was an authentic human being, born of a particular woman, given a specific name, living with identifiable family members in a known Palestinian community. He was indeed a known individual of history. Yet as people sought to understand him, they shifted in time from this historical Jesus to a Jesus who inspired faith.

The Jesus of history clearly had an influence on those around him. He had a band of followers, and reports were widespread of miraculous healings and exorcisms. He was a gifted teacher who engaged his listeners with stories related to the challenges and confusions in their own lives. Yet these factors alone would not have led to the extraordinary legends and myths that sought to explain his power. The climactic event that shaped the lens through which all other portions of Jesus' earthly presence were to be seen and interpreted was the final week of his life, culminating in his crucifixion and the Easter experience. In fact, between 25 and 40 percent of each of the four Gospels is focused on that final week.

It has been said that so powerful was the experience of those last days that the first Christians designed liturgies to reenact it. And at least one scholar has suggested that it was primarily for this purpose that the Gospels were written. Further, when the faith community gathered after Jesus' death, they selected a new member who had also been a witness to the last days to join the ranks of the remaining band of eleven apostles. Something incredibly powerful had happened in those final hours.

When an electrifying event occurs, individuals first experience it and secondly seek to understand it. Finally, an effort is made to explain it. This threefold exercise results in a development of mythology and folktales to reveal the truth of the actual experience. These are not in themselves the actual experience; rather, they are the symbols by which that experience can be understood. Further, these myths are always shaped by the history and culture of the peoples who recount them. It is with this understanding that the narratives of Jesus' birth must be read.

The framework through which Jesus was interpreted was that of a kingly God who sent a son who lived a full earthly life and after dying and returning to his father would serve as an intercessor for the human race. Yet this framework obviously violates the historical Jesus who was "born of a woman," who was "beset by weaknesses," who had no earthly political power, no wealth, no home, and who died a real death. Further, this Jesus did not fit any of the models of an expected Jewish messiah. Even his closest followers did not understand him to be the long-expected messiah. Certainly his words recalled were not characteristic of those of a powerful leader. Rather, he spoke of serving, of welcoming the poor and outcast, and of loving one's enemies. He fit neither the hero of Greek mythology nor the hoped-for messiah of Jewish faith.

After the Easter event, there was the inner realization by his followers that this Jesus reflected a new image of God. No longer were they to see God solely or primarily as a powerful and remote king ruling life from afar, but as the God in whom the poor and weak could find comfort and peace, and who was incarnate within humanity.

This vision was shared, however, in light of the culture of Jesus' followers. As the story progressed, Jesus was first the revelation of God, then he was understood as having been exalted to God's right hand, and finally it was Jesus himself who triumphed. The journey had moved from God's action to Jesus' action. Thus, the scandal of the cross came to be understood as the preordained vehicle by which Jesus was transformed from a suffering Jesus to a regal one.

It would not be long before the scandal of his birth would become an issue as well. The Jesus of history—born a nobody in a town from which no good was thought to come—would be given, perhaps six decades after his death, a miraculous beginning.

BIBLICAL READINGS

Hebrews 4:15	Luke 10:29ff.
Hebrews 5:2	Matthew 5:39
Deuteronomy 21:22–23	Matthew 5:4
Matthew 18:3	Matthew 5:44
Mark 10:31	Luke 23:34
Luke 22:27	1 Corinthians 1:18

NEW INSIGHTS

....

....

....

QUESTIONS FOR REFLECTION

1. Locate in the Gospels of Matthew, Mark, Luke, and John the chapters and verses narrating the last week of Jesus' life, his crucifixion, and his resurrection. Note the proportion of each Gospel that is devoted to this period. What do you believe to be the significance of this?

2. Read Acts 1:15–26. Why was Matthias selected to join the other apostles?

3. Describe or define "God." What experiences or circumstances have brought you to this understanding of God? Does your understanding agree with what you believe Spong has asserted in this chapter?

4. The word *myth* has been used several times in these pages. What does this word mean to you? Is this a word you would use to describe the birth narratives found in the Gospels? Why or why not?

ACTIVITY

Decide how you want to share with your correspondent the feelings you have had in reading this chapter. Write in your journal the letter you would send.

CHAPTER FIVE

THE DEVELOPMENT OF THE BIRTH TRADITION

SUMMARY

Over the centuries the Christmas celebration has become the favorite holy day in the church year. When the biblical story that initiated that celebration is analyzed in the cold light of contemporary science, New Testament scholarship, and common sense, however, the individual is left with an infinite number of unanswered questions. Yet, the tale has so captured our imaginings and desires that we continue to cling to it irrationally, despite the fact that these birth narratives should not be taken literally.

The earliest recounting of the Good News of Jesus did not include a birth story, and the narratives as we now have them were probably two distinct traditions that we have unconsciously blended into one tale. Mark, the earliest Gospel, begins with Jesus' baptism, and does not contain the nativity story. However, Matthew and Luke, written later, both add a birth narratives that, although they contain similarities, are full of inconsistencies. A document designated as Q, which may have been the earliest written material of the Christian community, was probably used by both the writers of Matthew and Luke as they penned their Gospels; this document, though, is not believed to have contained a birth story either. Thus, the two divergent birth stories of Jesus are most likely the result of unique material available to each author alone.

There are, unquestionably, similarities in the Matthew and Luke renditions of the birth story. Both identify the parents as Mary and Joseph, both record an unusual conception, and both place the birth in the same time period. But the differences are inescapable and incredibly numerous. For instance, the genealogies are incompatible, the shepherds and angels appear only in Luke, and the magi and the flight into Egypt are found only in Matthew. Certainly, both cannot be historically accurate. Perhaps, suggest biblical scholars, neither is. It is with this latter conclusion that Spong concurs.

The beginnings of Christianity sprang from the underpinnings of the first creed: Jesus is Lord. After Jesus' death, he was exalted—that is, brought in some way into the very being of God. In this primitive Christianity, as understood by Paul, there was no resurrection as a return to life: it was within the Easter story that the exaltation occurred. The resurrection/ascension was a single event. In the retelling of this proclamation that Jesus was Lord, the narrative increasingly was interpreted as two distinct events: resurrection and ascension. Separated from the original experience by decades, the Gospel writers transformed it yet further when they attempted to relate the two events to each other. Each solved the problem differently.

While Paul and the disciples had claimed that Jesus was Lord and that he was exalted as God's Son at the time of the Easter event, later writers moved the moment backward in time, first to Jesus' baptism (Mark), then to his conception and birth (Matthew and Luke). There were numerous models for such a miraculous birth. Many of the Greek and Roman deities had wondrous births, as did Krishna, Buddha, and, from the Hebrew Scriptures, Ishmael, Isaac, Samson, and Samuel.

The narratives of Jesus' birth, then, are not historical records. They are instead stories written by people of faith to explain the significance of an individual whose adult life transformed those whom he encountered.

BIBLICAL READINGS

Matthew 1:16, 20	Matthew 1:2
Luke 1:27, 32	Matthew 2:21–23
Matthew 1:20, 23, 25	Luke 2:21ff.
Luke 1:34	Romans 1:4
Matthew 2:33	John 20:19–23
Luke 2:51	Mark 1:11
Luke 3:38	Romans 1:4

NEW INSIGHTS

....

....

....

QUESTIONS FOR REFLECTION

1. Construct an abbreviated time line showing Jesus' birth and his death approximately thirty years later. Then place the following in that time line: Paul's writings (A.D. 49–62); the Gospel of Mark (usually dated A.D. 65–70); the Gospels of Luke (dated A.D. 80–85) and Matthew (about A.D. 90). What insights, if any, does this time line contribute to your understanding of the birth narratives?

2. Biblical scholars note that there was no known liturgical celebration of the nativity before the third century. Does this surprise you? Why or why not?

3. In your church, does the Christmas celebration overshadow the Easter liturgical celebration? In your opinion, what is the reason for this?

4. Spong asserts that the birth narratives, although not historical fact, can be seen as proclamations of the gospel. Further, assigning them to mythology does not mean in his view that they are untrue. What do you think he means by these statements?

5. In the past, when you recalled or recited the birth story of Jesus, how did you accommodate the differences that appear in the Gospels of Matthew and Luke?

6. Explain what the author meant when he said, "The designation of Jesus as God's Son had an almost inevitable backward trek in the understanding of the members of the Christian community as they groped to explain their experience with this special life" (p. 58). Read from the Gospel of John 1:1–5 (written at the end of the first century). Does this follow the above pattern?

7. Does it make any difference to you if Jesus became God on Earth at the time of his resurrection, at his baptism, at his conception, or at the beginning of time? Why or why not?

ACTIVITY

Write to your correspondent after finishing this chapter. Are there new ideas you want to share? What facts or insights most disturbed you?

CHAPTER SIX

MATTHEW'S STORY, PART I

SUMMARY

The Gospel of Matthew was written in the ninth decade follow-ing the birth of Jesus. This was after the fall of Jerusalem to the Roman army and at a time when the Gentiles in the fledgling Christian fellowship were becoming more numerous, resulting in the weakening of Jewish ties to the community. The anonymous author was probably a Jewish scribe who had become a Christian and who hoped in his writing to reveal the presence of the God he met in Jesus. And he undoubtedly felt that the Gospel of Mark, with which he was familiar, was not adequate for the age and community he inhabited.

In his writing Matthew conveyed respect for the scribes and Pharisees, but hostility for those religious leaders who opposed Jesus because he was challenging their legalistic interpretation of the Jewish law. Matthew saw Jesus as more concerned with the inner meaning of those laws. Thus, the Gospel writer not only desired those of Jewish heritage to see the folly of their narrow understand-ing of their laws but also wished the increasing gentile majority to recognize that the universalism seen in Jesus had its roots in Jewish history and traditions. It is with the use of midrash that Matthew seeks to reveal Jesus in the terms of the celebrated personages of Jewish history: Abraham, Joseph, Moses, Samson, for instance. Therefore, for Matthew it is important that the readers of his Gospel see Jesus as the son of David, the son of the Abraham mes-sage, and the son of God.

The Gospel drama opens with a genealogy of Jesus' ancestors, a list with many difficulties, including the inaccurate number of gen-erations cited and the inclusion of five women. The women—Tamar who pretended to be a harlot, Rahab who was a prostitute, Ruth who slept with her kinsman while he was intoxicated, Bathsheba who was impregnated by King David while she was married to

Uriah, and Mary—have been a fascination to biblical scholars through the ages. Some contemporary theologians see the first four women as a foreshadowing of Mary's compromised sexual status. To Matthew they illustrate how God could achieve his divine purpose despite a breach of moral norms. Thus, Matthew's genealogy alludes to the possibility that a bit of scandal surrounded the birth of Jesus.

Then the actual birth story begins. Mary was betrothed to Joseph (perhaps as a young teen), but before the beginning of their married life, a pregnancy occurred. Although this might have been condemned in some regions in Palestine, in Bethlehem of Judea where Matthew locates the holy family, the code was somewhat less stringent. The Gospel writer indicates, however, that there were some concerns about the pregnancy: perhaps Jesus was illegitimate; perhaps Mary was raped. In any case, Matthew has Joseph wondering whether to divorce Mary quietly.

In those early years of the Christian church when Matthew wrote, the concept of the Spirit was not as a distinct person of the Trinity, but rather as an expression of God identified with life and breath. Thus, he discerned the Spirit as a creative force, an agent by which God would empower a prophet to speak or the disciples to missionary zeal after the death of Jesus. This was not a Spirit understood to possess sexual prowess, and Matthew himself did not suggest that the Holy Spirit was the biological father of the child.

In developing his birth narrative, the writer returns again and again to demonstrating how the expectations of the Jewish Scriptures were accomplished in Jesus. Recalling a version of Isaiah 7:14, Matthew notes that "All this took place to fulfill what the Lord has spoken by the prophet." The passage he uses, translated from the original Hebrew, promises, "Therefore the Lord himself will give you a sign. Look, the young woman is with child and shall bear a son. . . ." However, when Matthew cited this verse to buttress his conviction that the birth of Jesus fulfilled an earlier prophecy, he used a later translation, probably from the Greek, which had "virgin" in place of "young woman." Thus a complication was introduced for generations of Christians to follow. Matthew surely used midrash in his interpretive assessment of this man Jesus, but later writers assumed that the Hebrew Scriptures were actually prophecies written centuries earlier to predict specific events in his life.

Stories of miraculous births were not uncommon in the Mediterranean region during the time Matthew penned his Gospel, and such tales probably circulated in the early Christian community as well. Perhaps Matthew used the Isaiah text to provide support for his proclamation that Jesus was not only of Davidic lineage but also the Son of God from the time of his conception. Thus Matthew provides a divine origin for Jesus and cleverly counters those who were suggesting that he was illegitimate.

BIBLICAL READINGS

Matthew 8:11	2 Samuel 11:2ff.
Matthew 3:9	Deuteronomy 22:23–27
Matthew 1:16	Isaiah 7:14
Genesis 38:1ff.	Matthew 1:23
Joshua 2:1ff.	Romans 1:4
Ruth 3:6ff.	Isaiah 11:1–2

NEW INSIGHTS

....

....

....

QUESTIONS FOR REFLECTION

1. Using a Bible dictionary if available, or a regular dictionary or encyclopedia if not, define the following words that are used in this chapter:

- dispersion (p. 63)
- Pharisees (p. 64)
- Gentiles (p. 66)

- Gnostics and/or Gnostic Gospels (p. 72)
- Septuagint (p. 74)

2. Count the number of generations that Matthew records in his genealogy (Matthew 1:2–17). How many did you find? Repeat this exercise with Luke's genealogy (Luke 3:23–38). What did you find? How do you explain this discrepancy? Spong notes (p. 68) that scholars think that the span of years encompassed is too great for this limited number of generations. Does this make a difference to you?

3. The inclusion of five women in Matthew's genealogy has bedeviled biblical scholars for years. Spong suggests that Matthew included them as a foreshadowing of Mary's compromised sexual status. Luther and Jerome earlier had indicated that the women's status as sinners or foreigners was the critical factor for Matthew. What theory might you put forth to account for their presence?

4. Using a map of Palestine at the time of Jesus' ministry, found in either your Bible or Bible dictionary, locate Judea, Galilee, and Bethlehem. Reread Spong's final paragraph on page 71 to find the importance of these settings.

5. Explain the difference between midrash and the concept of using ancient texts to predict literal events in Jesus' life.

6. Imagine that today you acquired some mystical ability to know for certain that Jesus was illegitimate or born of a violated woman. Would this be a problem for you? How would it affect your faith? Do you believe you would find it necessary to curtail publication of these facts? If you had lived in the first century and known this information, what methods or devices might *you* have used to diminish its impact?

ACTIVITY

This chapter may have contained some ideas that were new to you. Some of them may even have angered you. And you may have wished to dispute some of the facts or conclusions that the author presented. As you write to your correspondent, be certain to indicate the feelings you had as you read and contemplated this material.

CHAPTER SEVEN

MATTHEW'S STORY, PART II

SUMMARY

The remaining portion of Matthew's birth narrative is not any more literally true than were the tales of the pregnancy of a virgin, a questionable genealogy, and the angelic annunciation to Joseph noted in the previous chapter. The wondrous star, the traveling magi, the holy family's journey to Egypt, and the slaying of male babies by order of a king are as much an invention by the Gospel writer as the former sections were. They were, in fact, created with the express purpose of demonstrating that Jesus was not only the fulfillment of the Jewish Scriptures, but, additionally, the means by which the Gentiles could share in that tradition and gift.

The Jewish Christian author of Matthew used his own and his audience's familiarity with the Hebrew Scriptures to weave a story that none of them believed to be literally true. All knew that the narrative was Christian midrash, written to interpret the adult life of Jesus. New Testament scholars today continue in that understanding, debating not the literalism of the tale, but rather which of the Hebrew texts were actually the source for Matthew's tale.

Precursors for the magi, for instance, can be witnessed in several places. One contemporary scholar sees the background of this portion of the nativity story in Isaiah, particularly in chapter 49, verses 1 and 7, and in chapter 60, verses 3 and 6. Another New Testament scholar looks to the Balaam and Balak legend found in the Book of Numbers, chapters 22 to 24, as the primary source for this birth narrative tradition. And, finally, a third candidate for influencing Matthew's author can be observed in the 1 Kings tale of the Queen of Sheba visiting Solomon with gold, spices, and precious stones.

Midrash can also be discerned in the story of Joseph fleeing with his family to Egypt to escape a certain death for the infant Jesus at the hand of Herod. The earlier story—found in Genesis—

had another Joseph protecting his family from starvation by providing sustenance and a home in the land of Egypt as well. Likewise, the proclamation of Herod in the Matthew Gospel that he would kill all male babies under the age of two is an echo of the Exodus story in which a pharaoh sought to end the life of the one who was born to be the deliverer of the Israelites by slaying all Jewish male babies in Egypt. Moses, like Jesus, was saved by the ingeniousness of his family.

The star that appears in the Matthew birth narrative has many potential antecedents in the midrashic understanding of the Hebrew Scriptures, any of which may have been the source for the Gospel writer's use of this powerful symbol. Perhaps as likely a source for a wandering star, however, are two natural phenomena that occurred at approximately the time of Jesus' birth. The first of these was the appearance of Halley's comet. The second was the rare juxtaposition of three planets—Jupiter, Saturn, and Mars—so as to appear as one exceedingly bright star. Perhaps the Gospel account is a blend of the midrashic interpretation and the astrological events remembered by Christians seeking a sign to proclaim the fulfillment of the ancient promises.

Both Josephus and the Roman writer Pliny recount historical events that could have been the foundation for a Gospel story about magi visiting the infant Jesus. If, as Spong notes, magi from the east could come to pay homage to the Roman emperor Nero, how much more might they have come to pay homage to the King of Kings, the Son of God? Even the author of Matthew, however, does not furnish for his readers the number of magi who came to Bethlehem or identify their ethnic backgrounds. This has been left for later interpretation by the Christian church.

A final problem existed for the Gospel writer. How is he to explain the fact that Jesus is clearly identified with the village of Nazareth in Galilee, a city with no expected messianic associations and one mentioned pejoratively by Jesus' critics? Once again the midrashic method was employed and the obstacle was overcome by the crafting of allusions to the word *Nazarene* from the Hebrew Scriptures. Thus, we see, for instance, connections with both

Samuel and Samson, who were Nazirites—holy men who had been dedicated to the service of God. (Each, incidentally, also had an annunciation and birth story describing his beginning.) Further, the Hebrew word *neser* meant branch, and Jewish audiences would have had no difficulty understanding this as a reference to that messianic branch that was prophesied to come forth from Jesse.

The first two chapters of Matthew were not for the Gospel writer a biography of Jesus' early days of life. Rather, they were the author's attempt to claim for Jesus the fulfillment of the Hebrew Scriptures and a means to open that tradition so that the Gentiles could share in the gift of the Jews to the world.

BIBLICAL READINGS

Isaiah 49:7	Matthew 2:16ff.
Isaiah 60:3, 6	Matthew 2:20
Numbers 22–24	Exodus 4:19
1 Kings 10:1–13	Numbers 6:2
Matthew 2:2	Isaiah 4:3
Matthew 2:13–16	Judges 13:5
Exodus 1:15ff.	

NEW INSIGHTS

....

....

....

QUESTIONS FOR REFLECTION

1. The author of *Born of a Woman* claims that a literal translation of the infancy narratives is too fanciful for modern people to embrace. Do you believe this to be true? Are there any aspects of the story that would need to be literally true to sustain your faith? Which ones are they?

2. Using your Bible dictionary, read about the following persons mentioned in this chapter: Josephus (p. 92) and Jesse (p. 97).

3. From memory, answer the following questions about the magi:

    a. How many magi were there?

    b. Where did they come from and what was their ethnic background? What people did they govern?

    c. How did they travel?

Now read the entire episode of the magi as it is related in Matthew 2:1–18. How correct were your original answers? Where do you believe you have acquired the "facts" that you thought you knew about the magi?

4. On the map of first-century Palestine, found in either your Bible or the Bible dictionary, locate Nazareth in Galilee, Bethlehem in Judea, and Egypt, all locales where the Gospel of Matthew has the holy family living during Jesus' early years. Estimate the distances between them. What significance do you find in this information?

ACTIVITY

Write another letter to your correspondent. Be certain to record those things about which you have concern or disagreement with the author. Since the next three chapters will encompass the Lucan infancy narratives, you might also want to disclose in your letter your premonitions regarding the direction in which you believe the author will proceed.

CHAPTER EIGHT

BEHIND LUKE—AN ORIGINAL PAGEANT?

SUMMARY

The Gospel of Luke was in all probability written by the same person who wrote Acts; however, biblical scholars do not agree on the identity of this individual. Most likely he was a Gentile proselyte convert to Judaism and later a convert to Christianity. He certainly was a person comfortable with the Greek language, and, by implication from the prologue of the Gospel, not an eyewitness to the events he was recording. Clearly, one of his purposes in writing this Gospel was to assert that the mission of the Christian church to the Gentiles was part of God's preordained plan.

The author of Luke had before him the Gospel of Mark—as did Matthew when he wrote—and inserted into his document large portions of it. Some scholars suggest that since the text reads cohesively without the Marcan material, the original version of the manuscript did not contain it. They further theorize that the birth narrative in Luke 1 and 2 was also a later addition and the Gospel originally began with the third chapter. Some also suggest that Luke had access to the Q document (referred to in chapter 5) and/or to Matthew's manuscript, as well as to material that scholars have designated L, a source that was uniquely Luke's. Some of this material was probably in written form, some orally transmitted, and some Luke may have created himself. In any case, the birth narrative, at least, probably had an earlier life before Luke incorporated it into his Gospel.

The infancy story from Luke is far better known than its cousin in the Gospel of Matthew. The reason for this may be its possible origin as a drama performed for the early Christians and its continuing presentation in that form so that each adult today has seen its production countless times. In its present literary format, each vignette in the story in Luke is clearly separated by a device to change the scenes, and thus readers can envision a pageant enacted before their eyes. It is easy to imagine the entire production, because, in fact, it originally was a production, contends Bishop Spong.

The author postulates that in the beginning there were only four scenes: (1) the annunciation about John the Baptist with its theme from the Hebrew Scriptures of Abraham and Sarah; (2) the annunciation about Jesus with its theme from the story of Hannah in 1 Samuel; (3) the birth, circumcision, and naming of John; and (4) the birth, circumcision, and naming of Jesus. To this Luke added a few themes and the canticles. The viewers of this original drama did not interpret it literally but rather understood it theologically—i.e., that the adult Jesus had been identified with God from the moment of his conception.

BIBLICAL READINGS

Luke 3:1–3	Luke 1:80
Luke 1:23	Luke 2:15
Luke 1:38	Luke 2:39–40
Luke 1:56	Luke 2:52

NEW INSIGHTS

....

....

....

QUESTIONS FOR REFLECTION

1. Define the words *canticle* and *Magnificat*. Then, read the ancient story of Hannah from 1 Samuel 2:1–11 and compare Hannah's Song with the Song of Mary in Luke 1:46–55. What similarities do you find between Hannah's Song and the Magnificat in Luke?

2. Read the annunciation story of John the Baptist in Luke 1:5–25. Compare this with the annunciation story of Isaac found

in Genesis 17:15–21, Genesis 18:1–15, and Genesis 21:1–8. What significance do you place on their similarity?

3. If Luke's readers and the audiences of the ancient dramatic productions of Jesus' birth did not interpret the events portrayed literally, why do you suppose that Christians from the second century until the nineteenth century understood them in that way?

4. Locate in a hymnal or book of Christmas music four or five of your favorite carols. Read the words carefully and determine whether they are based more on the birth narrative as it is presented in Matthew or in Luke.

ACTIVITY

Write once again to your correspondent. If you have discovered new insights or meanings to the Lucan birth story, share them in your letter. Indicate whether they are helpful to you or confusing. And if you have questions that disturb you, include them as well.

CHAPTER NINE

LUKE'S STORY, PART I

SUMMARY

The first portion of Luke's Gospel has as its heart the interplay of two people: John the Baptist and Jesus. In the early years of Christianity there appeared to be no rivalry between the two movements that developed around these individuals; yet as time passed, a clear need emerged to subordinate the personage of John to that of Jesus. This was accomplished by interpreting John's witness as the one that prepared the way for Jesus.

Although some members of the embryonic Christian church desired to identify John the Baptist with Elijah, the founder of Jewish prophecy, the author of Luke was not among them. He chose to portray Jesus as the new and greater Elijah, with John as the individual who prepared the way for Jesus without being aware of his critical role. In later writings in the Book of Acts and the Gospel of John, the subordination of John is even more emphatically recorded.

It is through his parents, Zechariah and Elizabeth, that we are introduced to John, and Spong speculates that it is through the use of midrash that we are able to understand the role these individuals will assume in the birth of Jesus. For instance, both of their names hearken back to celebrated Hebrew people from earlier centuries whose lives contained similarities to their own.

In the opening scene in Luke, the priest Zechariah is chosen by lot to enter the temple to offer incense and while there is visited in a vision by Gabriel, who tells him that his prayer has been heard, that his wife's barrenness will be overcome, and that a son will be conceived. Zechariah leaves the temple after this annunciation dazed and mute from disbelief. Yet despite the angel Gabriel's promises, John is portrayed in Luke as being subordinate to Jesus in every way.

Whereas a vision in the Book of Daniel story appears to be the backdrop for the annunciation to Zechariah of John's birth, it is the tale of the barren Hannah found in 1 Samuel that can be discerned from the annunciation account to Mary. And it is within the meeting of Mary with the angel Gabriel—and only there—that the idea of the virginal conception is found in Luke.

The virgin birth tradition is not essential to the remainder of Luke's story, and modern-day biblical scholars wrestle with the reasons for its inclusion. One speculation is that it was incorporated into the drama in an effort to demonstrate further that Jesus was greater than John the Baptist, for whereas Elizabeth conceived in the barrenness of her old age, Mary conceived without the benefit of a human father for the child. This would indeed proclaim Jesus' superiority over John the Baptist.

A second possible explanation for the inclusion of a virgin birth story in Luke was the necessity felt by the early church to answer critical speculation about Jesus' origins. Thus a defense of his birth became a crucial task to blunt the attack of enemies and persecutors of the new Christian church. In several places the author of Luke makes it clear that Joseph was not the father of Jesus, and John the Baptist (as an adult) notes that God did not need Jewish paternity to raise up children to Abraham (Luke 3:8).

Was it possible that the birth of Jesus was encircled by such scandal that only a supernatural birth tradition could counter it? Perhaps Mary was seduced, violated, raped? Wouldn't the creation of such a birth narrative establish not only that Jesus was greater than John the Baptist, but that even through a child born outside impeccable Jewish lineage God's will could be accomplished? Unquestionably, that would have been a miracle to first-century believers.

After both annunciation stories are related in Luke, Elizabeth and Mary meet while Elizabeth is pregnant. The reader is informed that the baby leapt in Elizabeth's womb and she was filled with the Holy Spirit, exclaiming to Mary, "Blessed are you among women and blessed is the fruit of your womb! And why has this happened to me, that the mother of my Lord comes to me?" (Luke 1:42–43). Here follows the canticle called the Magnificat sung (or said) by Mary, and like the other canticles in these early chapters of Luke, it appears to tie portions of the drama together and give voice to those who may have been acting in pantomime. These canticles have very Jewish roots and were probably not written by the author of Luke but rather adapted by him.

After Elizabeth gives birth to her son, he is named by the mute Zechariah, who writes the name on a tablet. As his speech miraculously returns, Zechariah breaks out in a canticle of prophecy that has been called in Christian writings the Benedictus. Here Zechariah prophesies of John, "And you, child, will be called the prophet of the Most High; for you will go before the Lord to prepare his ways . . . " (Luke 1:76). The concluding words of the canticle have been interpreted to extend God's family beyond its Jewish roots: "By the tender mercy of our God, the dawn from on high will break upon us, to give light to those who sit in darkness and in the shadow of death, to guide our feet into the way of peace" (Luke 1:78–79).

Thus the interpretative pageant continues. Already we see that it was created to authenticate the adult lives of both John the Baptist and Jesus, and to subordinate John to Jesus in the Christian community.

BIBLICAL READINGS

Luke 7:19	Mark 3:31ff.
Malachi 3:1ff.	Luke 8:19–20
Exodus 6:23	Luke 1:66
Daniel 8:16ff.; 9:21ff.	Luke 7:26
Luke 3:15–16	

NEW INSIGHTS

QUESTIONS FOR REFLECTION

1. The author of *Born of a Woman* notes that it was important for the early Christians to expand their understanding of those who were to be included in God's family (p. 126). Why do you believe this might be true?

2. List as many similarities as you can between the birth and life of John the Baptist and the birth and life of Jesus that emerge in these first three chapters of Luke. What significance do you attribute to the list you have compiled?

3. Reread the two paragraphs that begin on page 126 with the words "It was important to those early Christians . . ." and end on page 127 with the question "Is it possible that Mary was a violated person and that people referred to her as 'the virgin' who had been raped so that Mary the Virgin became the way people thought of her and the name by which they called her?" How would you respond to that final query?

4. Do you believe it is possible—if perhaps only remotely— that Jesus was conceived by the Holy Spirit? What does the word *conceive* mean to you? How would you answer those who argue that if Mary was not impregnated by the Holy Spirit, then Jesus was not divine as claimed by our Christian faith?

5. The Nicene Creed, regularly recited by Christians, contains the following passage: "For us and for our salvation he came down from heaven: by the power of the Holy Spirit he became incarnate from the Virgin Mary, and was made man." What does this mean to you?

ACTIVITY

This chapter may have presented ideas that you found disturbing or that challenged your faith. As you write to your correspondent this time, be certain to share these problem areas and explain the reasons for your feelings. Include in your letter those things you would ask the author if he were present.

CHAPTER TEN

LUKE'S STORY, PART II

SUMMARY

After encountering Jesus in their lives, the earliest first-century Jewish Christians struggled to find ways to explain their extraordinary experience. Searching their Jewish Scriptures, they located numerous passages they felt could be understood within the context of the life and ministry of Jesus and their association with him. Looking at portions of Isaiah, the Twenty-second Psalm, and Micah, for example, they found suggestions that not only helped them interpret the meaning of his life, but helped them remember what they thought had occurred. Later, many of these same readings would be used to claim for Jesus a "fulfilling of the Scriptures." All of this evolved before the Gospels were committed to written form, and in Luke we see evidence of the midrash tradition that was employed by these earliest of Christians.

The author of Luke faced several challenges in writing his birth narrative: he wished to portray Jesus as the fulfillment of all that the Hebrew Scriptures required for the messiah; he desired to place Jesus in a status above that of John the Baptist; and he wanted to make clear to the Roman community that Christianity was not a political threat to their government. He managed this by placing Jesus' birth in Bethlehem, not only to fulfill the Jewish messiah expectations, but also to indicate a location superior to John the Baptist's anonymous birthplace and to show to the Romans that this was a law-abiding family that obeyed the decrees requiring tax enrollment.

This incredible revelation of God had to be witnessed in some way or it would not have been revelatory. Whereas the author of Matthew used magi to respond to the revelation, Luke used shepherds. Until that moment when the angels appeared to the shepherds, only Mary and Elizabeth and possibly their husbands were aware of the momentous event that had occurred. That this had come to pass in the city of Bethlehem was crucial for Luke: this was the home of the shepherd David, ancestor of Jesus, who left his flocks to become king of Israel. Some scholars suggest, using the midrash approach, that a passage from Micah with its images of Bethlehem and childbirth shaped the traditions of Luke. The angelic message to the shepherds outside Bethlehem would be carried to Mary and eventually would become the message to the world.

After Jesus' birth he was brought to the temple in obedience to the Jewish law. The rite of presentation and the rite of purification were actually two rites that Luke confused in his birth narrative by blending them into one. Both had as their root various texts from the Hebrew Scriptures found in the books of Exodus, Numbers, and Leviticus mandating that the firstborn child be consecrated or dedicated to the Lord and that the mother after childbirth be brought to the temple for the required purification. In this story, as Simeon prepares to bless Jesus and his family, we are able to detect clear images from the presentation of Samuel, centuries earlier, to the old priest Eli in the temple.

Guided by the Holy Spirit, Simeon prophesied by way of a canticle—known throughout Christendom as the Nunc Dimittis—that Jesus would be ". . . a light for revelation to the Gentiles. . . ." Whether this canticle had as its source verses from the latter portion of the Book of Isaiah or came from the Jewish Christian community known as the Anawim is debated by scholars, but it is certain that Luke had Simeon articulating the position that Gentiles would hold in this new kingdom. A second prophecy came from Simeon at this time: that Jesus was destined to be a stumbling stone for many in Israel while for others a cornerstone. And, he concluded, a sword would pierce Mary's own soul as well. A dark and menacing shadow had fallen on the holy family.

The Christmas pageant appears to be over at this point suggests Bishop Spong. Yet Luke has included one further episode in his narrative. This is the story of Jesus returning to the temple for Passover with his parents when he was twelve. At that time he seems to be aware of his origins and his future role in Israel. This self-knowledge at a young age is analogous to Daniel's self-awareness at the age of twelve in the Book of Susanna. It, like much in the Gospel of Luke, could be the midrashic tradition once more at work.

The author of Luke never intended this birth narrative to be literal historical fact. In all probability, states Spong, Jesus was born in Nazareth in a very normal way to Mary and Joseph, or else he was born as an illegitimate child who was validated by Joseph when he acknowledged him as his son. There were no angels, no shepherds, no journey to Bethlehem. The "truth" in this glorious story is that God has drawn near to us in the person of Jesus.

BIBLICAL READINGS

Luke 2:22–24	Luke 2:11
Luke 2:4, 11	Exodus 13:1
1 Samuel 16:10ff.	Leviticus 12:1–4
Micah 4:9–10; 5:2–3	Isaiah 49:6
Isaiah 9:5–6	Luke 2:39

NEW INSIGHTS

....

....

....

QUESTIONS FOR REFLECTION

1. Who were Herod the Great, Quirinius, Caesar Augustus, and Theophilus?

2. Spong notes that early in the history of Christianity several sections of the Hebrew Scriptures were used to understand the life of Jesus. One of these was Psalm 22. Read this psalm. Why do you believe it is used today in so many Christian churches during Palm Sunday and Good Friday services?

3. How would you explain to a friend or acquaintance the following quote from page 138: "Far from 'fulfilling the Scriptures,'

as the Christians once claimed, the ancient Scriptures actually determined the way people told what they thought they remembered"?

4. Spong argues that many of the ideas he presents concerning a literal understanding of the Scriptures in general, and the birth narratives in particular, are commonplace among biblical scholars, yet are all but unknown among average worshipers in churches and synagogues in the country (p. 140). Do you agree with him? If so, why do you believe that this is true?

5. Explain the phrase used several times in this chapter, "christological moment" (see, for example, pp. 146 and 156). After having read *Born of a Woman* to this point, when would you contend that this moment occurred? Why?

6. What does Spong mean when he indicates that Luke was not a careful historian?

7. Write down six or eight things you believe about Jesus. Now outline a birth narrative you might write that would validate your beliefs.

ACTIVITY

Once again, compose a letter to your correspondent. Have you made any startling discoveries about yourself, your beliefs, your responses to challenging ideas? Share them as you write.

CHAPTER ELEVEN

BIRTH HINTS FROM MARK AND JOHN

SUMMARY

Of the four Gospels, only Matthew and Luke contain birth narratives. Yet both Mark—the earliest Gospel by ten to fifteen years—and the last Gospel, John, penned at the turn of the first century, have clues to Jesus' family as well.

Bishop Spong suggests that an extremely contentious relationship between Jesus and his family is revealed in the Gospel of Mark. This can be observed in several passages. For instance, Jesus' family comes to restrain him because they fear he is "out of his mind," and he responds to the crowd, "Who are my mother and my brothers?" Later he notes that prophets are not without honor except in their hometown, and among their own kin, and in their own house.

Several other verses could be interpreted as possibly presenting an autobiographical note. In one of these passages, Jesus uses the illustration of a person coming to plunder a strong man's property after binding the owner of the house. Could these verses convey a message about his own conception, asks Spong. In a later chapter in Mark, someone in a crowd calls Jesus "son of Mary," an uncommon, perhaps shocking, appellation for an honorable man in Palestine at that time. Since Joseph is never mentioned in Mark, there is a possibility that this designation was meant to convey an illegitimacy surrounding Jesus' birth. Further, when Jesus speaks of the human family unit in Mark, he repeatedly omits reference to a biological father.

The Gospel of John, written near the close of the first century, is also devoid of a birth narrative. Despite the fact that birth stories about Jesus were widely known by this time, the writer of John chose not to include one. Instead, this Gospel begins by placing Christ at the beginning of time: "In the beginning was the Word, and the Word was with God, and the Word was God. He was in the beginning with God. . . . And the Word became flesh and lived among us, . . . full of grace and truth." Throughout his Gospel John depicts Jesus ridiculing those who would take his words literally. Perhaps he therefore placed in his Gospel a theological interpretation of Jesus that would defy literalization. Unfortunately, over the years, the opposite has occurred.

Also in this Gospel, Jesus makes a distinction between physical and spiritual births, implying that there was no contradiction to the concept that one could be born of God's Spirit and through normal human conception as well. Nicodemus, a Jewish leader with whom Jesus was conversing, was obviously quite confused by this.

Mary appears only twice in John. The first is in the wedding story that takes place in Cana of Galilee where she is concerned about the wine. Here Jesus rebukes her with, "Woman, what concern is that to you and to me?" She does not reappear until the crucifixion scene. Jesus' brothers are also shadowy figures, seen only once—and that time in a mocking reference by Jesus when they question his actions. The biblical editorial response is, "For not even his brothers believed in him." The separation between Jesus and his family in this Gospel mirrors the separation and discord found in Mark.

After the dialogue with his brothers, Jesus went to the Feast of Tabernacles in Jerusalem, where a noisy controversy arose around him concerning who he was and whence he had come. In the midst of this dispute there is a story of a woman taken in adultery. Once again the question is raised by the author of *Born of a Woman* about the possibility of this episode's autobiographical origins.

The comments of the crowd become increasingly hostile, until an assertion by one of those present is noted: "We are not illegitimate children. . . ." And the name-calling continues. This portion of John concludes with yet another hint of Jesus' birth. The story of the man born blind was an opportunity for the disciples to ask Jesus if the blind man himself had sinned or his parents. Neither, Jesus responds, but that the works of God might be revealed in him. Again it is not difficult to find an allusion to Jesus' birth in these verses.

Over the years, the church has transformed the challenge of Jesus' crucifixion into a symbol of life. It is time that this same church looks at the scandal of his birth and sees in it the power of hope as well. "If God can be seen in the least of these, our brothers and sisters, as Jesus suggested, could not God also be seen in the infant of a violated woman who needed the protection of a man in order to survive in a patriarchal world?" asks Spong.

BIBLICAL READINGS

Mark 3:25   John 2:4

Mark 10:30–31   John 8:41

John 1:14   John 10:30

John 3:4, 5, 6

NEW INSIGHTS

....

....

....

QUESTIONS FOR REFLECTION

1. Add the writing of John's Gospel to the time line you created in chapter 5. Does this give you any new insights?

2. Why do you believe the authors of Mark and John did not include birth narratives in their Gospels?

3. Read Mark 3:20–27 and determine if you would analyze it in any way other than the one Spong suggests on page 162. Repeat this exercise for Mark 3:31–35, which Spong interprets on page 163.

4. Explain what you believe Spong means when he asserts that there has been a gradual dehumanization of Mary in the history of the Christian church (see p. 167).

5. Read John 1:1–5, 14. Explain in your own words what you believe these verses mean. How does the writer of John's

Gospel differ in his understanding of Jesus from the writers of Matthew and Luke? Note that the *Word* ("logos" in Greek) can be understood as "God in action," i.e., Jesus is this *Word*.

6. Do you recall the verses from John 1:1–5, 14 ever being used in Christmas liturgies in your church? Why do you believe they have been included?

7. Read the seventh and eighth chapters of John. Comment on your feelings after you have finished.

ACTIVITY

As you write your letter to your correspondent after completing this chapter, be certain to include your areas of agreement and disagreement with the author of Born of a Woman. *There were many biblical references in this section that could be interpreted in a variety of ways. You may have found Spong's suggestions convincing and helpful or difficult and debatable. As you write, remember to inform your correspondent of the emotions you felt as you read.*

CHAPTER TWELVE

FACING THE IMPLICATIONS OF SCRIPTURE

SUMMARY

The ancient baptismal creed of the Christian church contains the phrase "conceived by the Holy Spirit and born of the Virgin Mary." These words, like others in the creeds, attempt to explain an encounter the early Christians had with their God through Jesus. And, like all such attempts, the creed contains truths that can never be completely revealed by words alone. When literalized, these creedal concepts may become analogous to a straitjacket that confines—one that needs to be broken apart in order to find new meaning for those in the church of today. It is impossible for Christians to defend the religious tradition of their past unless that faith is open to change, to growth, and to new meaning. The literalizing of words and symbols guarantees death.

For two thousand years the church's elders have struggled against those who would seek new truths. In the past the pioneers of such ideas were put on trial for heresy, imprisoned, deposed, even burned at the stake. Today the battles continue, but the victims are faced instead with harassment, ridicule, and occasionally deposition. The church persists in tolerating its fundamentalist members (traditionalists) but attacks those who explore new roads and are open to new truths.

It is possible for the believing Christian to recite the creeds with integrity despite the fact that they contain phrases such as "conceived by the Holy Spirit and born of the Virgin Mary." The virgin birth narratives point to profound religious truths: first, that in the divine–human encounter, the initiative always comes from God; second, that the people who had been with Jesus recognized that they had experienced the presence of God in him, and that human life alone could never have created the power he possessed. The symbols from the birth narratives can strengthen our belief that in the life, love, and being of Jesus we see the life, love, and being of God. It is indeed possible to accept the meaning behind the symbol without having to accept that symbol literally.

Jesus makes numerous references to God as Father in the four Gospels. By examining these various references, one may assume that an image of how Jesus perceived earthly fatherhood had emerged. If this is true, then a picture of Joseph comes into focus that is not only caring, but a powerful source of love, protection, and strength. Of particular note is the parable of the prodigal son in Luke. Here can be seen a portrayal of a father who cares deeply for his lost son and rejoices upon his return while at the same time recognizing the demands of an elder brother that the traditional inheritance laws be observed. It is not difficult, notes Spong, to imagine an autobiographical theme here.

In other verses Jesus speaks of a father who showed the son all that he was doing and of one who transferred his power to his son so that both were honored together. Jesus claims that he speaks as the father has taught him, that he is one with the father, and that he lives because of the father. Could not this oneness and love be referring to both his earthly and his eternal father? It is possible that Joseph's relationship with Jesus was one of such profound power and beauty that it shaped the growing child's understanding of the father God— a God that he called "daddy." This becomes even more powerful and compelling if Jesus was indeed the child of a violated woman, a child whom Joseph adopted and nurtured as his own. Assuming this is the case, then Joseph's relegation to relative obscurity by both the Gospels and the church has been a grave injustice.

BIBLICAL READINGS

Mark 10:7	Luke 15:32
Mark 7:10; 8:38	John 5:19
Matthew 8:21	John 5:20
Matthew 11:27	John 8:44; 14:13
Matthew 7:11	John 5:26
Luke 6:36; 8:51; 11:11, 13	John 17:1

NEW INSIGHTS

....

....

....

QUESTIONS FOR REFLECTION

1. Words and symbols are an attempt to give expression to an experience. Examples of symbols might be the word *God*, a cross, a dove, the scarlet letter *A*, advent wreaths, and wedding bands. Name as many other symbols—religious or secular—as you can within five minutes and note what each of them signifies. Would you describe your experience or understanding of these symbols in the same way as another person might? Why or why not? Does this make the symbol any more or less valid or valuable? Why?

2. Spong notes that "Creedal phrases always look backward to their origins as well as forward beyond their limits" (p. 173). What does this mean? Do you agree with him that the real enemies of a faith system are not the "tradition benders" but the "tradition freezers"?

3. Why did the church condemn Galileo and Copernicus? Have you witnessed or read about any similar reactions by contemporary church authorities to unfamiliar or unorthodox ideas?

4. Read the Apostles' Creed or the Nicene Creed. Underline those phrases that you are unable to accept literally. If you repeat these creeds weekly, how would you explain to an acquaintance that you recite them but do not believe them? Do you believe it is possible to take these symbols seriously but not literally, as Spong suggests? What does that mean?

5. Are you convinced by the evidence offered in this chapter that Joseph was Jesus' paradigm for "father" from which he was able to understand God? Why or why not?

6. Spong offers one plausible hypothesis to those who question why Joseph's position in the Gospels and in the church has been virtually eradicated. Are you able to provide any other possible explanations?

ACTIVITY

Bishop Spong developed two major themes in this chapter: first, he examined the place of symbols in our understanding of theological truths; and second, he investigated the possible role that Joseph played in the development of Jesus and his concept of God the Father. Include in your correspondence your feelings and ideas about both of these issues as they were presented by Spong.

CHAPTER THIRTEEN

SUPPOSE JESUS WERE MARRIED

SUMMARY

Both Jesus and his mother, Mary, have been dehumanized in the writings, theology, and tradition of the Christian church—partly as a consequence of the principal interpreters of this history being celibate priestly males. One of the ways in which this dehumanizing has occurred has been the outright discouragement of any questioning of the possibility that Jesus was married.

Although no indisputable claim of marriage is made in the Gospels, there are innumerable clues that could definitely be interpreted in that way. Furthermore, throughout history there has been a continuing undercurrent of speculation that Mary Magdalene and Jesus were romantically linked. Surprisingly, much negativity surrounds such a theory—as if the condition of marriage would be less than exemplary for the God-man.

For the alert reader, though, hints abound in the Gospels that could support the theory that Jesus was indeed married. For instance, in several texts it is noted that women and wives accompanied the disciples in both Galilee and Judea. In many of these references Mary Magdalene is specifically mentioned and always, when she is with other women, is given the priority position. In first-century Palestine, the status of women was related to the status of the men with whom they were linked. It is possible to argue that since Mary Magdalene was always noted first that she was in some way related to the primary person in the Gospel accounts, i.e., Jesus.

In the four resurrection recordings, Mary Magdalene is the only woman mentioned in each one as being at the tomb. In the Gospel of John she is portrayed as calling Jesus "my lord," and in speaking to the gardener she offers to claim the crucified body—highly unusual for a woman unless she was next of kin. John also notes that when Mary recognized Jesus at the tomb, she embraced him. Yet in

Palestine society of that time women did not touch men unless they were married.

Two other stories hold clues that could support the hypothesis of a married Jesus. The first, the wedding feast in Cana of Galilee, hints of the possibility that Jesus was the bridegroom—that was the reason his mother was so concerned about the expended wine supply. The second, the Mary and Martha story, takes place in Bethany and includes the intimate portrait of Mary anointing Jesus' head with oil and kissing his feet—actions that would be appropriate only for a wife or perhaps a prostitute. The weight of evidence would appear to support the former: Mary was Jesus' wife.

A tradition has developed over the years that claims Mary Magdalene was a prostitute; however, there is no biblical evidence to support this assertion. This accusation may have been prompted by the need of the church to remove her from primacy in Jesus' life and replace her with the sexless virgin mother. Spong suggests that the reason for this is the historical negativity of the church toward women, which defines them as the source of sin, the polluter of otherwise moral men. The only perfect woman according to church thought—and the definition by which all women were thus measured—was seen in the person of the mother of Jesus, the virgin mother Mary.

BIBLICAL READINGS

1 Corinthians 9:1ff.	John 20:1ff.
Mark 15:40	John 20:15
Matthew 27:55–56	Luke 10:38ff.
Matthew 27:61	Mark 3:31–35
Mark 16:1	Luke 8:19–21
John 1:49	

NEW INSIGHTS

....

....

....

QUESTIONS FOR REFLECTION

1. Reconstruct in your own words the argument that Spong uses to support his speculation that Jesus was married and that his wife may have been Mary Magdalene. Do you find this plausible?

2. Reread the story of the wedding in Cana of Galilee (John 2:1–11). Are you able to suggest explanations other than the one Spong offers for Mary's concern about the wine?

3. Would you find either Jesus' divinity or his humanity diminished if he were known to have been married? Why or why not?

4. What do you think Spong meant when he wrote that the primary vehicle through which the definitions of women have entered Christianity has been the figure of the virgin Mary (p. 198)? Do you agree or disagree with his contention that women have been *victims* of this tradition? Why or why not?

ACTIVITY

As you write the letter to your correspondent, include your ideas on whether the author's arguments for his theory are cogent and convincing. Note also how you feel about the possibility that Jesus may have been married. Will it make a difference to your faith?

CHAPTER FOURTEEN

THE COST OF THE VIRGIN MYTH

SUMMARY

The Judeo-Christian faith story has been a major source of the negative view of women throughout the centuries. The religious and cultural consequence of the Bible's interpretation by men has been the inevitable oppression of women that continues yet today. Beginning with woman's subordinate place in the creation myth and progressing to the birth narratives in which a virgin gives birth to the Savior, a picture is painted of the perfect woman: docile, obedient, and powerless.

As the Christian faith took shape, it embraced many of the patriarchal views of the society in which it evolved. Thus no female deity was included in the Trinity as that theology developed. Instead, there was a male God, his male son, and the Holy Spirit—traditionally thought of as a masculine figure as well. Attempts by groups such as the Gnostics to represent the Spirit as feminine resulted in the thundering call of heresy by the orthodox Christians. The feminine vacuum was ultimately filled, however, with Mary the mother of Jesus. Despite the fact that Mary Magdalene appeared as a much more powerful figure in the drama of Jesus' life, by the second century it was Mary the virgin who had won the day. The result was an image of a woman that was to be the model for all women for centuries to follow: obedient, faithful, cooperative, and sexless, as opposed to the lusty, strong, and powerful love model mirrored in Mary Magdalene.

As the early Christians attempted to define the Jesus of their faith, they battled those who would deny his humanity. The result was the growing significance of his birth—"born of the Virgin Mary." Mary, now an integral part of this defense, also had to be defined. Employing the Pauline concept of Christ being the new Adam, some theologians found an analogy with Mary and Eve.

Whereas Eve turned away from God, Mary was obedient and received God—"Be it unto me according to your will." Eve was sexual and evil. Mary was sexless and good.

Virtue for the early church fathers became identified with virginity, and undergirding this concept was the assumption that the flesh of a woman was evil. Virginity became the higher calling and marriage was but a compromise with sin for the weak. In fact, by the later years of the second century, the idea that Mary was a perpetual virgin, unsullied by even married love and sex, was added to the tradition of the church. Gone was the concept of the goodness of God's creation.

The teachings of the fifth-century Christian Augustine, the bishop of Hippo, added to the myth that surrounded Mary. Indeed, the sinlessness of Jesus depended upon Mary's virginity since evil, the sin in life, was transmitted through sex. It was this theology that dominated Christian thought for fifteen centuries and provided the climate for the next steps in the march of divinity for Mary. In the middle of the nineteenth century the dogma of the Immaculate Conception was proclaimed—i.e., she was "preserved immaculate from all stain of original sin...." Finally, within the last fifty years of the current century, the dogma of the bodily assumption of Mary at her death was promulgated by the Roman Catholic church. This Mary, without humanity or sin, was heralded as the perfect woman. Yet no woman could hope to emulate her.

The church proclaimed in myriad ways that sex was evil except as a means of perpetuating humankind. And the sexuality of women was the most evil since it was the source of male desire. In this charged atmosphere, resulting at least partly as a consequence of the birth narratives of the early church, women continued to be denigrated. The Protestant Reformation has helped to dislodge these views of women that developed in the church, and in those countries where the rebellion against traditional Christianity was most complete, a new definition of women and a new status for women have emerged.

As the clamoring of twentieth-century women for elimination of sexist attitudes in the church continues, the institution will find it imperative to respond in order to survive. In time, this will bring a redefinition of God, of Jesus Christ, and of Mary. At that time we can "again worship and adore the God who is met in the heart of our humanity incarnate as male and female."

BIBLICAL READINGS

1 Corinthians 15:22	Mark 3:31
1 Corinthians 15:47	Galatians 1:19
Genesis 4:1	Ezekiel 44:2
Genesis 3:16	John 20:19–23
John 7:2	John 2:5

NEW INSIGHTS

....

....

....

QUESTIONS FOR REFLECTION

1. Spong describes a working woman's employment as dependent upon a man's willingness to hire her and on her ability to please her male boss (p. 202). As such, working women were powerless. Does this describe your experience or the experience of those working women you know?

2. Not all the consequences of the birth narratives and the myth of the virgin Mary have been negative. Two positive consequences are noted on page 203. Are there others you would add to these?

3. Spong asks, "What would have been the shape of Christian theology and history if birth narratives had never been included in the writings of Matthew and Luke?" (p. 204). How would you answer him?

4. Have you ever thought about the fact that there is no distinctly feminine aspect of the Trinity? If so, how did this make you feel? Do you imagine that your answer might be different if you were a member of the opposite sex? Why or why not?

5. Take a few minutes to write down all the attributes you can think of to describe Mary Magdalene. Repeat this exercise for Mary, mother of Jesus. What insights come to you as you look at the lists you have created?

6. Christian theologians have struggled over the centuries to define both Mary and Jesus. To see the scope of these views, write a sentence about the beliefs of each of the following people or groups:

- the Docetists (p. 208)
- Valentinus (p. 208)
- Iranaeus (p. 209)
- the Manichaeans (p. 211)
- Augustine (p. 217)

7. What does the author mean when he describes Mary as "a male-created female figure who embodies the kind of woman dominant males think is ideal" (p. 221)?

8. Do you agree or disagree with the following statement: "Belief in the virginity of Mary is not necessary for an individual to possess a belief in the divinity of Jesus"? How would you support your view in a dialogue with someone who answered the question differently than you did?

ACTIVITY

This chapter has been designed to support the contention that ideas do indeed have consequences. Spong contends that the biblical birth narratives along with the virgin Mary myth have had a significant effect on the church and the culture of the past two thousand years. As you write your last letter to your correspondent, share your feelings about this concept, as well as any unanswered questions you have after completing the book.

CONCLUSION

You have now completed *Born of a Woman: A Bishop Rethinks the Birth of Jesus*. A few final tasks remain in order for you to determine if your objectives in reading this book have been accomplished.

1. Return to the beginning of your Study Guide and look through the New Insights you noted from each chapter. Do you believe you were led to many new ideas, facts, or understandings in the reading of the book? Mark those that were most meaningful to you. Did you find as many of these new ideas or discoveries in the biblical readings as you did in the pages of *Born of a Woman?* Was this a surprise? As you look at the New Insights from the fourteen chapters and compare them, do you note any patterns or any areas where you might choose to continue reading or to initiate personal research?

2. Look at the first entry in your journal and read the list of goals you noted before you started the book. How many were achieved? What might have been changed by either you or Bishop Spong to satisfy more of your expectations?

3. Now spend some time looking through the letters you wrote in your journal as you completed each chapter of the book. The purpose of this Study Guide activity was to enable you to articulate your feelings about the highly provocative material that Spong was presenting. In some cases, it was expected you might even encounter some of your own biases or prejudices. As you reread these entries, do you find the earlier ones similar to or different from those you wrote later? How would you explain this? What have you learned about yourself? For instance, how do you react to ideas that challenge your values? If you found yourself in a debate on the issues of biblical literalism, the value of midrash in understanding the Gospels, or the effect of the birth narratives and the elevation of Mary on the status of women, what would be your stance? Do you think reading *Born of a Woman* has changed any of your views? Reinforced them? Having read this book and worked through the accompanying Study Guide, would your recommend it to someone else? Why or why not?

BORN OF A WOMAN

The intent of the following section is to assist a leader in designing a six-week course for use with a group of adults interested in reading and discussing *Born of a Woman*. The material has been adapted to conform to the traditional one-hour Christian education time schedule available in many churches on Sunday mornings; however, if the group is meeting at another time, it is recommended that seventy-five to ninety minutes be allocated for each session.

PURPOSE OF THE COURSE

Since John Shelby Spong hoped that *Born of a Woman* would elicit dialogue and debate on the issues he raised, this course is designed to have participants

- read and understand the author's major arguments and the supporting biblical passages
- be aware of both new insights they have gained and feelings or biases they carry to any dialogue on this provocative material
- be able to articulate their own views in either support of or opposition to those presented in the book

These goals are to be accomplished by a multifaceted approach involving short presentations by the leader, small discussion groups, and journal writing. Limited homework is also recommended.

GATHERING THE PARTICIPANTS

Before the first session, the leader should bring together those adults who have expressed an interest in participating in a six-week course. Each person should be able to get a copy of the book or, alternatively, the leader should arrange to obtain copies for the group.

Because these sessions will not be designed as lectures, it is essential that participants commit themselves to reading the designated material before each class meeting. The leader should also request at this time that each person bring to the classes a notebook that can be used as a personal journal, a New Revised Standard Version of the Bible, and a pen or pencil. (If desired, the leader can suggest that each person purchase a copy of the Study Guide, although this is not a necessity. In any case, the following pages are written with the assumption that the participants will *not* have personal copies of the Study Guide. Minor adaptation of the directions by the leader is required if all participants will have their own copies.)

The time and date of the first meeting should be announced and the first assignment given at this introductory gathering. It is recommended that a schedule of the meeting dates, a list of the necessary materials, and the first assignment all be prepared in advance and distributed at this time.

IDEAS FOR CREATING A HEALTHY GROUP ENVIRONMENT

1. The meeting place should be as comfortable and spacious as possible, allowing participants to meet in both small and large groups.

2. The purpose of each session should be clearly stated and all agendas and time frames noted. Ideally, newsprint could be prepared with this information before the start of the class and be in view as participants arrive.

3. An environment of trust is essential if all members of the group are to participate in the various discussions in the six meetings. In order for this to occur, individuals should value other members of the group and listen to their views despite the strong possibility that they may find themselves in disagreement. Each person should be treated with dignity and respect and all opinions treated with seriousness. All group members should have an opportunity to contribute to a discussion, and no one person should be allowed to dominate.

4. Either the leader or a participant assigned to the task should open and close each meeting with an appropriate prayer.

5. The leader or co-leaders should arrive at each session well prepared and on time. The meeting room should be inviting and ready, with the necessary materials on hand. It is also recommended that a few reference books be available, if possible, for questions that may arise during the discussion periods. A map of the Palestine of Jesus and a Bible dictionary such as *Harper's Bible Dictionary* are suggested as a minimum. Newsprint with the purpose of the day's session should be on display. All sessions should start and end at their appointed times.

6. Last, it is recommended that the leader prepare in advance written copies of all assignments for each participant—both for homework and for in-class group discussions.

ASSIGNMENT TO BE DISTRIBUTED TO ALL CLASS MEMBERS BEFORE THE FIRST MEETING

1. Read all introductory material and chapters 1 and 2 of *Born of a Woman*.

2. Using the New Revised Standard Version (NRSV) of the Bible, read all biblical passages noted in these two chapters.

3. Divide your journal or notebook into two equal parts. Label the first section "New Insights" and the second "Feelings, Reactions, and Responses." Note in the New Insights portion any new information or understandings you have acquired in the assigned reading—both book and Bible. Write in the second section of the journal a short letter to register your feelings about the material you have been reading. Address it to someone you know well—a family member or friend. It can be a person whose religious views are similar to yours or else dramatically opposed. It may help to imagine the person sitting across from you in your living room. What would you say? Do you agree with what you have just read? Disagree? Are you angry? (Keep in mind that you will *not* be sharing this portion of your assignment with anyone in the class unless you choose to do so. This is your personal response to the material you are engaging.)

4. Answer the following question: If, as the author claims, the Bible is not free of contradictions and historical and scientific inaccuracies, of what value is this collection of books that Christians call sacred Scripture?

WEEK 1

Purpose

- To acquaint class members with the format of the six-week course
- To examine the difficulties of using a literal understanding of the Bible
- To note the value of using the midrashic method to interpret the stories from the Bible
- To begin work with journals

Introduction and Prayer
(10 MINUTES)

1. Open class with a prayer.

2. Indicate objectives for both the complete six-week course and week 1 of the course.

3. Write on newsprint the format that will be followed for this first day, with times inserted.

4. Have group members introduce themselves. Note that they will be working with one another in small, changing groups over the next weeks.

5. Ask for volunteers for opening and closing prayers for weeks 2–6.

Presentation
(10 MINUTES)

Leader summarizes the material in the first two chapters and allows for a short period for questions or comments.

Discussion
(20 MINUTES)

Break the class into small groups with four persons in each. Their assignment in these groupings is to discuss the following: (1) What new insights or information did you gain in either the home reading or the leader's summary? (2) What was the most problematic or challenging material for you in this section? (3) How would you as a group answer the question you were assigned for this first week? (4) Finally, as leader, select two questions from the reflection questions found in the Study Guide in chapters 1 and 2 and have the groups react to one you have chosen from each chapter. Be certain one question deals with the concept of midrash.

A recorder for each group should prepare a short response to each of these five questions.

Summary
(10 MINUTES)

Return to the large group and have the recorders place on newsprint the answers their groups developed to the questions. The leader should comment on similarities and differences he or she discerns in the responses.

Journal
(5 MINUTES)

Provide time for participants to add to either or both sections of their journals as a result of this hour meeting.

Assignment
(5 MINUTES)

Hand out the following assignment for the next session.

1. Read chapters 3, 4, and 5 in *Born of a Woman* and any biblical references that are included.

2. Enter in your journal the "New Insights" that have come to you as a result of your reading. Also write a short letter in your

journal to the person you have chosen as your correspondent. Include in this letter your feelings and reactions to the material in these three chapters in the section labeled "Feelings, Reactions, and Responses."

3. Answer this question: Do you believe it is possible that Paul knew of a miraculous birth and yet did not include it in any of his writings? Of what significance is this? If he did, what might this imply about the significance of the birth story to Paul? If he did not, of what significance is that to a study of the birth narrative?

Closing Prayer

WEEK 2

Purpose

- To examine Paul's understanding of Jesus' birth
- To explore the connection between Jesus' life and death and the birth narratives that developed
- To note some of the differences in the birth narratives as reported in Matthew and Luke
- To discover the historical development of Mark, Matthew, and Luke

Opening Prayer

Presentation
(15 MINUTES)

Leader presents a summary of material in chapters 3, 4, and 5 and allows a short time for questions and comments. This is also an appropriate time for the construction of an abbreviated time line on newsprint to give a sense of the historical framework. Show the following events: Jesus' birth and death; Paul's writings and death; and the appearance of each of the Gospels of Mark, Matthew, and Luke in written form.

Discussion
(25 MINUTES)

As you did last week, break into groups of four persons. Have the membership of these groups as different as possible from the previous session. Give them the following assignment, asking them to report to the large group with a short response for each question. (1) What new information did you discover in these three chapters? (2) How did you answer the home assignment question? (3) The term *myth* was used several times in these pages. Is this a word you would use to describe the birth narratives? (4) In the past when you recalled or recited the story of Jesus' birth, how did you accommodate the differences that appear in the Gospels of Matthew and Luke? (5) What implications come to you after viewing the time line constructed earlier in the class?

A recorder from each group, preferably a person who has not had an opportunity previously, should be ready to share the group's comments.

Summary
(10 MINUTES)

Return to the large group and have the recorders place on newsprint the answers their groups have developed to the questions. When all have finished, the leader should comment on areas of agreement or disagreement.

Journal
(5 MINUTES)

Provide five minutes for participants to add to either or both sections of their journals as a result of this session.

Assignment
(5 MINUTES)

Hand out the following assignment for the next session.

1. Read chapters 6 and 7 of *Born of a Woman* and all the biblical references.

2. Write in both sections of your journal as before.

3. Imagine that today you had some mystical power to know for certain that Jesus was illegitimate or born of a violated woman. Would this be a problem for you? How would it affect your faith? Do you believe you would find it necessary to curtail publication of this information?

Closing Prayer

WEEK 3

Purpose

- To explore Matthew's purpose in writing his Gospel message
- To become acquainted with Matthew's presentation of the birth narrative and his use of midrash

Opening Prayer

Presentation
(15 MINUTES)

Leader summarizes the material in chapters 6 and 7 and allows sufficient time for comments and questions.

Discussion
(25 MINUTES)

Once again, divide the class into small groups of four, trying to place people as much as possible in different groupings. The four tasks to be completed are: (1) List new data or knowledge gained by members of your group in this section of the book. (2) How did your group answer the homework assignment? (3) Using your Bibles, decide which aspects of the birth story in Matthew are best explained for you by the midrashic technique. (4) Are there any elements of Matthew's story that need to be literally true for you to sustain your faith? What are they?

Each group should have a recorder prepare a short response to each of these questions.

Summary
(10 MINUTES)

Return to the large group, where recorders will place on newsprint the answers their groups have prepared. When all have completed this task, the leader will respond with observations.

Journal
(5 MINUTES)

Provide a few minutes for participants to add to their journals any new insights or feelings they may have realized during this session.

Assignment
(5 MINUTES)

Distribute the following assignment for the next session.

1. Read chapters 8, 9, and 10 of *Born of a Woman* and all biblical references. Note: This is the longest assignment in the six-week course.

2. Write in both sections of your journal.

3. Locate in a hymnal or book of Christmas music four or five of your favorite carols. Read the words carefully and determine whether they are based more on the birth narrative as presented in the Gospel of Matthew or the Gospel of Luke.

Closing Prayer

WEEK 4

Purpose

- To envision the birth narrative of Luke as a dramatic performance

- To recognize the connection between John the Baptist and Jesus in the Gospel of Luke
- To consider the possibility that Jesus' birth was accompanied by scandal

Opening Prayer

Presentation
(15 MINUTES)

Leader summarizes the material in chapters 8, 9, and 10, allowing sufficient time for comments and questions.

Discussion
(25 MINUTES)

Divide the class into groups of four, once again trying to place them with people with whom they have not worked. Each group should answer the following questions: (1) What new insights have you gained in reading these three chapters? (2) How did you answer the homework assignment? (3) The Nicene Creed, regularly recited by Christians, contains the following passage: "For us and for our salvation he came down from heaven: by the power of the Holy Spirit he became incarnate from the Virgin Mary and was made man." What does this mean to you? (4) What is your reaction to Spong's suggestion that Mary's pregnancy may have been the result of rape or adultery?

Have a recorder, if possible someone who has not had the task before, ready to share with the large group a short response to each of these questions.

Summary
(10 MINUTES)

Return to the large group and have the recorders place answers developed in their groups on newsprint. The leader should be ready to comment as before.

Journal
(5 MINUTES)

Provide time for participants to add to both sections of their journals as a result of this session.

Assignment
(5 MINUTES)

1. Read chapters 11 and 12 of *Born of a Woman* and all biblical references.

2. Write in both sections of your journal.

3. Read the Apostles' Creed or the Nicene Creed. Underline those phrases that you are unable to accept literally. If you repeat these creeds regularly, how would you explain to an acquaintance that you recite them but do not believe them?

Closing Prayer

WEEK 5

Purpose

- To examine the hints in the Gospels of Mark and John about Jesus' earthly family
- To consider the place of symbols in our understanding of theological truths
- To explore the possible role of Joseph in the development of Jesus and his concept of God the Father

Opening Prayer

Presentation
(15 MINUTES)

Leader summarizes the material in these two chapters and allows a short period for questions or comments. Included in this presentation should be the placement of the writing of John's Gospel onto the time line created in week 2.

Discussion
(25 MINUTES)

Divide the class into four-member groups, giving them the following assignment: (1) Did you discover any new information in these two chapters? (2) How did members of the group answer the homework question about the creeds? (3) Why do you believe the authors of Mark and John did not include birth narratives in their Gospels? (4) Do you agree with Spong that the real enemies of a faith system are not the "tradition benders" but the "tradition freezers"?

A recorder for each group should be prepared to give a short response to each question.

Summary
(10 MINUTES)

Return to the large group and have the recorders place on newsprint the answers their groups have developed. The leader will react to similarities or differences in the responses as appropriate.

Journal
(5 MINUTES)

Allow a few minutes for participants to add to their journals as a result of this session.

Assignment
(5 MINUTES)

1. Read the last two chapters of *Born of a Woman* and all biblical references.

2. Write in both sections of your journal.

3. Would you find either Jesus' divinity or his humanity diminished if he were known to have been married? Why or why not? Why do you believe it might have been a problem for the early Christians?

Closing Prayer

WEEK 6

Purpose

- To examine the possibility that Jesus was married
- To consider the effects of the church's elevation of the Virgin Mary on the status of women
- To evaluate the course

Opening Prayer

Presentation
(15 MINUTES)

Leader summarizes the material in chapters 13 and 14, allowing a short period for questions or comments.

Discussion
(25 MINUTES)

Break the class into four-person groups and give each the following assignment: (1) How did members of your group answer the nomework question? (2) Divide the men and women in your group, and respond to this exercise: List the attributes of the ideal woman as you believe women would respond. Now list the attributes of the ideal woman as you believe men would respond. How similar are the responses for the two groups? Are they similar to or different from the ones the author claims the church has perpetuated? (3) How different do you think Christian theology and history would have been if birth narratives had not been included in the writings of Matthew and Luke?

Recorders should be prepared to present their small groups' reactions to these questions.

Summary
(10 MINUTES)

Return to the large group and have the recorders place on newsprint the answers that their groups have developed to the questions. The leader should be prepared to comment as appropriate.

Journal
(10 MINUTES)

Provide time for class members to reread their journal entries for the past six weeks. Have each person write on a sheet of paper a statement about his or her learnings and/or self-discoveries as a result of reading *Born of a Woman*. It is not to be signed, but placed in a box anonymously, so that leaders can later evaluate course success.

Closing Prayer